THE ADVENTURES OF QUINTEN

Quinten Visits the Beach

A Story About Coping with Autism

AUTHOR: NIKKI C.

The Adventures of Quinten
Quinten Visits the Beach
A Story About Coping with Autism

ISBN: 978-1-7361360-0-3

Copyright © 2020 by CNJ Books & Publishing LLC

Written By: Nikki C.

All rights reserved. No part of this book may be used or reproduced in any manner whatsoever without the prior written permission of the author.

This book is dedicated to my very brave son Quinten and all the brave children coping with autism. You are different not less.

"Quinten, are you ready to go to the beach?" Mama asked excitedly. Quinten jumped up happily and screamed "Yeah!" He was always eager to go on an adventure, even if he was not sure where he was going.

As they approached the beautiful tan sand that led to the ocean, Quinten froze immediately, and his eyes raced from left to right.

"No, No, No!" He shouted as he snatched his hand away from Mama's grip.
How do I get to the beach without touching the sand, he thought.

He turned to his Mama and said, "Up please".
Mama knew that Quinten needed support until he could adjust to this new environment. She picked him up and carried him through the beautiful tan sand towards the beach.

As they got closer to the beautiful blue ocean, Quinten and his family found the perfect spot to set up their beach umbrella.

Dad set it up while Mama continued to hold Quinten as he studied everything around him.

After Dad laid the blanket out under the umbrella, Quinten sat down on the blanket and eagerly began pulling his beach toys out of the bag.

He sat at the edge of the blanket playing in the sand with his pail and shovels.

Mama stood up and began to head towards the beautiful blue ocean. "Quinten would you like to come with Mama to get in the water"? she asked.

Quinten stood up too and shouted "Yes"!
She picked him up and carried him through the beautiful tan sand to the cool water.

At first Quinten played happily in the water, with Mama swirling him around in the beautiful blue ocean. Then came a big wave out of nowhere and crashed beside them unexpectedly.

I do not want to be in the water he frantically thought and began clinging tightly to his Mama's neck.
"No, No, No," Quinten cried out.
How do I get out of the water? He asked himself.

Quinten turned to Mama and said, "I want Daddy". She then put Quinten on her back and carried him through the beautiful tan sand towards Dad who was seated under the umbrella.

Dad sat Quinten on the blanket under the umbrella, but he moved to the edge of the blanket to play with his beach toys in the sand.

He laughed happily as he put sand in his pail and emptied it out again and again.

Mama stood up and looked towards the beautiful blue ocean.
"Quinten would you like to go back to the water with Mama"? she asked.

I do not want to go back to the water,
he anxiously thought as he began to flap his arms up and down.
"No, No, No," Quinten cried out.
What can I do to stop Mama from taking me back to the water? he thought.

Quinten turned to Mama and said, "All done, home please", and Mama picked him up as Dad began to pack everything so that they could go home. When they were all packed up, Mama carried Quinten through the beautiful tan sand again, towards the car.

After one hour of fun in the sun, Quinten's day at the beach had come to an end.

He did not enjoy walking in the sand or being in the beautiful blue ocean, but he had fun at the beach and that was enough for him.

He loved playing with his beach toys in the sand under the umbrella.
He also enjoyed looking at the beautiful tan sand as Mama carried him through it.

Quinten had to find out what worked for him in this new environment. Once he figured it out, he experienced the beach in a way that was fun for him.

Made in the USA
Columbia, SC
05 December 2020